So,
Are the Skies Really Gonna Part?

In His service,

Dale Goodrich

Phil 4:13

So,
Are the Skies Really Gonna Part?

Dale Goodrich

REDEMPTION ◖ PRESS

Dedication

This book is dedicated to my wife Susan, son Logan and daughter Jillian. Their dedication, love and support have meant more to me then they'll ever know.

Susan, your sacrifices have not been acknowledged by the same medals, ribbons and insignia that I get to wear on my Air Force uniform so the average person on the street doesn't know what you've been through. Our Lord and Savior Jesus Christ, however, has seen it all! Your love over the years and those tearful prayers on 9/11 have meant more to me than words could ever say!!

Logan, I've been able to comfortably go about my business because I know I've got another man in the house to look after things. I couldn't possibly tell you how proud you've made me throughout your life. You are an outstanding young man after God's and my own heart. Keep up the great work!

Jillian, you are my ever present ray of sunshine. After a long hard day in the rat race, I know one of the first things I'm going to see when I come through the door is that trademark smile of yours that absolutely lights up the room. I couldn't imagine one single day without your sweet, heartfelt love!

Acknowledgment

The very first person to whom I want to offer my thanksgiving and praise is my personal Lord and Savior Jesus Christ. The words on these pages are His. Thank you, Jesus, for allowing me to be your mouthpiece!

I want to thank several dear friends and associates whose input was absolutely vital as this work took shape and moved towards completion. A fresh perspective and willing intellect are terrible things to waste. I thank God that He put people in my life who were willing to share theirs with me.

My neighbor and dear friend, Peggy Hart, is an inspirational mentor and gifted student of our Savior. Her guidance and editorial comments were laser focused and right on the mark. Thank you Peggy!

My good friend, Norm Kolb, has a sharp eye for the Lord and was extremely helpful with thoughts, suggestions and general theological guidance. Norm, your gentle spirit is a precious gift that He has given me through you. My friendship with you is something I will always cherish!

I am honored to call Campus Crusade for Christ evangelist and author Randy Newman ("Questioning Evangelism," Kregel Publications, February 1, 2004) my friend. It seems like everyone who knows him can never get enough of his "down to earth" style and wise counsel. I count myself among those who feel that way. I could blissfully spend countless hours soaking up his perspective. Randy, to say you've been an inspirational friend would be a gross understatement. Thank you for your help!

My boss at United Airlines, Captain Walt Clark, is a man with whom I've formed precious memories during heartwarming, insightful conversations about our Lord. It was his perspective on the horrors of Hell that were so useful in writing the chapter on that subject. Walt, your wise leadership and unwavering guidance in the face of the company's darkest hours have touched lives in ways you'll never know. Thank you for your friendship!

My Air Force Reserve boss, Mr. Carl Mc-Cullough, is the ultimate class act. Sir, I will always remember my service under your leadership as one of the true highlights of my military career. It has been an honor and a privilege to work by your side and to see, firsthand, what it means to labor with a servant's heart. Thank you for the thoughts you shared on this work and the way in which you've touched my life.

Our family often jokes that my "baby" sister, Lisa Laufer, and I are identical twins born nine years apart. It's almost spooky to see how similar our personalities really are. Lisa, you are one of the most beautiful, devoted Christians I've ever known. Thank you for being my spiritual sounding board. You're the best little buddy a big brother could've ever hoped for and your loving support over the years have meant more than you'll ever know. May God bless you!!

Table of Contents

CHAPTER ONE

The Attack

Tuesday, September 11, 2001 started out like every other Tuesday I'd ever encountered. It was a beautiful, quiet day and I was taking a break from my fulltime job as a pilot for United Airlines in order to fulfill my part-time military obligation as a Colonel in the Air Force Reserve. My duties on that particular day placed me in the National Military Command Center (NMCC) at the Pentagon. Little did any of us know, as we swung our feet out of bed that morning, that it would be a day whose impact would be felt for the rest of our lives.

While on duty in the NMCC, it was my job to keep tabs on any logistics related issues my boss may have needed to know about as various military operations played out around the world. The brave young men and women of the U.S. military are in harm's way in lots of places besides the Middle East, so those of us back at headquarters can be busy from time to time lending support. As this particular Tuesday dawned, I wasn't terribly busy. That was just fine, because my master plan was to finish several projects during what I'd hoped would be a quiet block of days. Actually, that plan was working well until I happened to look over at another officer and noticed that he and two colleagues were intently staring at the TV above their desks. Out of curiosity, I walked over to see what had them so enthralled. Images of smoke pouring out of one of the World Trade Center towers filled the screen. I made a beeline back to my desk and tuned in the news on my own set.

CNN's resident aviation expert was speculating as to what may have happened. One of the first comments I heard was "We think an airplane may have hit the tower...maybe even a commercial sized, twin engine jet." The exact cause was obviously still unknown. Even though the weather in NYC was perfect, the expert was asked whether or not a navigation malfunction could have caused the problem. Commercial flights are virtually always flown according to a plan that *could* be executed solely by reference to instruments in the cockpit. But anybody flying on a clear day like that would be doing so primarily by looking outside, so an instrument malfunction was out of the question.

I was anxiously waiting to hear whether or not an airline was involved. Not long afterwards, I overheard an officer on the phone say something about American Airlines. As horrible as this event was, I have to admit I breathed a small sigh of relief to know that, at first glance anyway, my United Airlines family didn't appear to be involved. The pace of conversations in the complex was picking up, so my attention was directed to several different places. Just then, I happened to look at the TV screen as the second airplane slammed into the other tower with the resulting fireball.

Shortly after the New York City part of the disaster played out, somebody in our work area reported that a hijacked aircraft was heading for Washington D.C. I had the incredibly helpless sense of being in the middle of a situation that was spiraling out of control and wanting to be able to do something about it. The Pentagon is obviously big and has a very unique shape that makes it easy to identify from the air. There was no reason, however, to assume that we had a significantly higher chance of being hit than any other high value target in the D.C. area. All of that notwithstanding, however, I felt unusually exposed and vulnerable. Shortly thereafter, those feelings became real in a shocking way when I heard a distinct, muffled, double BOOM. Actually, it wasn't as ear shattering as one might think. It was more like a massive industrial sized air conditioning unit kicking on, but obviously too loud to be that. Someone came in from a few offices over and said, "This building just moved!" Oddly enough, I didn't feel the building move. I only heard the noise.

Within a short time, many of the folks who worked in offices right above us began to filter downstairs for two reasons: situational awareness tools were in the NMCC and smoke was starting to ease into their workspaces. Within a matter of just a few moments, the building's alarms began to sound, directing everyone to evacuate. Surprisingly, we never did leave the building. The NMCC is pretty well environmentally controlled. Surgical masks were handed out, though, in case we ever had to leave the immediate area. The smoke just outside our office complex was thick enough that it was uncomfortable to breathe, but not dangerous. That alarm continued to blare for hours. On several occasions, I silently cursed the guy who designed it because, so far as I could tell, it didn't appear to be possible to turn the alarm off in those parts of the building where people didn't intend to evacuate. I just wanted to be able to hear myself think instead of listening to a continuous warning telling me to get out.

A short while later, someone else reported that another hijacked airplane had just crashed. By this time, I honestly began to wonder whether or not I was witnessing the end of the world. All I could think of was Tim LaHaye's description in his book *Left Behind,* wherein vehicles of every sort start crashing because their Christian drivers, pilots and engineers had been taken up into heaven when Jesus Christ came back to rapture His church. The only reason I knew that wasn't happening was the fact

16

that I was still here. Thanks to a very short prayer of salvation I'd recited in High School, my life has been in the palm of God's mighty hand ever since. I have fire insurance. It isn't insurance against the type of fire those terrorists caused that day. It's the kind you can only get by hopping up off the throne of your life and inviting Jesus Christ to have a seat! I know this may come across as a little presumptuous to the average non-Christian out there, but if airplanes start crashing because of the Rapture, I'll be watching that scene play out from within His tender loving arms instead of a smoky section of the Pentagon. That is His promise and I believe it with every bit of my soul.

It was quite surreal to watch news reports of the Pentagon burning while knowing that I was standing in the building being featured on TV. It was like starring in a live movie and simultaneously being part of the audience as well. The other extremely unsettling notion that began to descend on a few of us in the complex centered on the possibility that another aircraft, for all we knew, was headed for our location as well. After all, two were used to attack the World Trade Center towers—why not two on their target of choice in Washington, D.C.? We just didn't know. Every so often, eyes seemed to meet in a silent stare that begged for an answer as to whether we would be hit again, and possibly killed, or left to live another day.

I went into the conference room occupied by the One-Star General in charge, just to see if his team knew anything else that I didn't already know. Just as I walked in, things were getting quite busy. Various bits of official conversation, like "U.S. under attack from the air," and other similarly menacing things permeated the atmosphere. Conference calls could be heard on overhead speakers and the full might of the U. S. military was stirring to life. I immediately thought this had to be a nightmare, and that I would wake up any minute.

Not long after witnessing all of that, I became aware that my hands and feet were beginning to shake, my heart seemed to be racing, and my breathing was coming in short, rapid bursts. I was beginning to feel the onset of mild physical shock. That should not have come as any big surprise, given everything we were going through. Leaving the conference room, I was suddenly overwhelmed by the desire to have a very intimate conversation with God. It was almost like He was tapping me on the shoulder. For the first time in my life, I was confronted with the reality that I truly might not live through the day, so, to put it simply, I commended my soul to Him. It was not a matter of giving up—just an acknowledgment that He might be calling me home. Basically, I told Him I was ready to come quietly. Right on the heels of that conversation, however, He acquainted me with an aspect of my walk with Him that still needs some work. Every single one of us will leave loved ones behind and/or dreams unfulfilled when we die. I found it very hard not to dwell on that as I contemplated what my fate might be that day. I have to learn to trust God more fully for absolutely every single aspect of my existence, including the part where my body will eventually cease to exist. None of us will ever be made to take on more than we can bear. Knowing that my wife and children might actually have to lean on that promise, while not necessarily uplifting, certainly was instructive.

I really don't know how long the intimate time that God and I shared with each other lasted—probably no more than a minute or two, and perhaps shorter than that. It didn't end in any particularly noteworthy way. I just came out of my reverie and got plugged back into what was going on. To stop my hands and feet from shaking, I concentrated on slowing down my breathing and maintaining control, but at one point I did have to go sit down for a few moments. I tried to convince myself that I just needed to calm down and focus on the tasks at hand. I wouldn't be much help to anyone if I had to use up all of my energy just trying not to fall down. Again, it was a little surprising to experience symptoms of physical shock, but all of that just reminded me that being a Christian doesn't guarantee a life free from fear. It just guarantees that we won't confront it alone.

Approximately thirty more minutes of activity had passed when an unusually pronounced hush settled over the immediate area. Just then, I looked up and saw the Secretary of Defense, Mr. Donald Rumsfeld, enter the complex with his entourage.

Ever since I'd begun my assignment on the Joint Staff, I'd wanted to meet some of the military brass, and now here was the full show. Eventually, several four star generals including the Chairman of the Joint Chiefs of Staff, General Shelton, showed up as well. By now most of our efforts were centered on setting up a CAT (Crisis Action Team). This separate team of military personnel was preparing to work in a large complex of cubicles positioned quite a ways from the NMCC where I'd been during the actual attack. It is at this point that I believe a true miracle occurred for my wife, Susan. Shortly after the Pentagon was hit, I tried to call her to make sure she knew I was OK. As relentless as that effort was, I could not get an outside phone line. A coworker had gotten a line and was on the phone with his wife. He offered to have her contact Susan and let her know all was well. I obviously jumped at the offer and gave him my home phone number. A few minutes later, we made eye contact from across the room and he gave me a "thumbs-up," indicating contact had been made. I immediately put my thoughts of the home front on the back burner. A few hours later, I was at work in one of those CAT cubicles. I don't know how many workspaces were in this complex, but I was one among hundreds busily answering phones and reacting to the emergency. Until we could figure out who everybody was and where he or she was sitting, our standard operating procedure whenever a call came into the complex was to hold up the handset and yell the name of the person that the caller needed to reach. If within earshot, that person would then come over and take the call. After having been in the CAT for all of five minutes, the officer in the cubicle *right next to mine* held up his phone and yelled my name. That surprised me, because nowhere near enough time had elapsed for anyone to know that I'd been moved into the CAT. I took the phone and, in a very business-like manner said "Colonel Goodrich." I then heard my poor, frantic wife tearfully say, "Your voice never sounded so good!" I don't know whom my coworker's wife had actually called several hours before, but it obviously wasn't Susan. In desperation, after trying every number she had on an old recall roster I'd given her, she found one more number labeled "Crisis Action Team" and that one just happened to land her right next to me! Needless to say, I felt terrible. Those hours must have been torturous!

Sometimes, I think the families of military members are the ones who fight the toughest battles. I know that when the roles are reversed and my wife goes out for the day while I stay at home, I like to have some idea as to when she expects to return. Then, if she's not back by that time plus or minus five minutes, I normally go into full-blown panic mode. How she has managed to come to grips with the fact that her husband's whereabouts are, more often than not, a complete unknown to her is beyond me. Be that as it may, on that day God heard her cries and miraculously put us in touch. He also provided me with a very valuable lesson that He'd begun during our intimate conversation a few hours before. I mentioned that I was somewhat overwhelmed by the idea that my family might have to cope with the news of my death. He illustrated to me that I wasn't even capable of making a simple phone call, let alone living my family's life for them after I die. He miraculously took care of letting my wife know that I was OK. I believe He gave us that miracle in order to show me that I just need to trust Him! He is a God who is more than capable of seeing to every little detail of every life He's created, from coping with the death of a loved one to completing a simple phone call! The remainder of the day was filled with the type of work anyone would imagine has to be done after a disaster like this. Airlift requests had to be handled, and disaster relief efforts were getting underway. The rest of the day and night were not nearly as newsworthy as the morning had been.

As I look back on this disaster, I can't help but wonder whether or not these attacks have won more souls for Jesus Christ than anything else possibly could have. I can't even imagine how dark and over-whelmingly foreboding our new-world order must look to anyone who is trying to face it without the light of the Risen Christ showing them the way. Let's face it. One of the features of our way of life that we all hold so dear is freedom and our enemies have figured out how to use that against us as a weapon of mass destruction. They've also demonstrated that they have absolutely no qualms about doing so at any time or in any place. We humans are powerless to return this world to the simpler thing that we thought it was on September 10th. Many of the soldiers we're attempting to engage have lived right next door to us for years, because our system has wanted them to feel free to come here and do so. Right after the attacks began, the FAA grounded all air traffic in the country. How many of those grounded airplanes had hijackers on board? We'll never know, because if there were any, they simply got off their respective airplanes and drove back home.

Now we're dealing with everything from bio-terrorism to power plant security. The Secretary of Defense himself said that it's impossible to defend every conceivable target that could be hit. In other words, virtually every direction this discussion takes ends in hopelessness if we remain determined to use human ingenuity as the solution. Our national leaders are ordained by God to defend us, and that's exactly what they are doing, to the best of their collective abilities. There is no ultimate solution, however, apart from Him. We have only one way out of this nightmare and that is the Triune God—the Father, Son, and Holy Spirit. We can't solve this, but He can. September 11, 2001 was not, in fact, the end of the world, so it's safe to assume that He has a solution in mind and a plan for each one of us who were allowed to survive. We just need to have faith. Isaiah 55:8, "For my thoughts are not your thoughts, neither are your ways my ways, declares the Lord".

There has never been any doubt in my mind that I was *called* to pursue aviation, my love for it has been so intense. At one time in my life, however, my job as an airline pilot was a large part of my identity. That's no longer true. I used to think that God introduced me to my insatiable love for aviation when I was five years old because He knew that this world would need one more pilot someday and He wanted me to be that pilot. I now believe that He put me here because He knew the aviation world was going to need one more Christian someday and He wanted me that be that Christian. I also believe that my having been on duty in the Pentagon that day was His gift to me as well. My Air Force Reserve job occupies a small enough percentage of my total life that my having been there on that day feels a lot like part of His master plan for my life. I believe it was God's way of giving me an effective attention-getting step to use in my attempts to spread the good news of salvation through faith in Jesus Christ. I certainly don't want any looks of admiration for having been there.

What I do want, though, is the opportunity to help folks know that God wants to have a *personal relationship* with every single individual who doesn't already enjoy one with Him. My most heartfelt prayer used to be that I'd get to keep flying and eventually retire comfortably. The prayer is no less heartfelt now, but it's a prayer that everyone who reads these words or hears my voice will come away knowing the name Jesus Christ. If you've never asked Him to come into your life and take control, He's knocking on your door even as we speak. Your next opportunity to claim His gift of eternal life could be your last. I sincerely doubt that any of the victims who died on September 11th woke up that morning and said, "Yup…today's the day…I guess I better get to know the Lord!"

CHAPTER TWO

Setting The Stage

As you just saw, my experience in the Pentagon, however unlikely it was for me to have even been there in the first place, was defined, in large part, by what transpired many years before when I became "born again." Exactly what does it mean to be "born again" and why should you care? As my story continues, I am going to attempt to shed some light on those questions in a way that provokes both thought and, hopefully, action. If you're not already "saved," "born again," or whatever you want to call it, you are the one for whom I wrote this book. In a sense, you're reading a sales brochure. Our Lord and Savior, Jesus Christ, is obviously not for sale. He is, however, someone you can most definitely *choose* whether or not to "consume." He even tries to drive home that point by inviting us to His eternal table in John 6:35. "Then Jesus declared, 'I am the bread of life. He who comes to me will never go hungry, and he who believes in me will never be thirsty'".

Before we even get started, though, I would like to clear up any confusion that may exist with regard to terminology. I've already thrown quite a bit of it out there, having used such labels as "saved," "born again," and "Christian." Some of them are even officially defined in dictionaries. I saw one once that defined the term "born again" and concluded with the phrase "born-again Christian." That caught me by surprise, because strictly speaking, that's an incorrect use of the term. That's like calling a young woman a "female girl."

If you were to stand outside any Christian church on a Sunday morning and, as folks file out after the service, ask them whether or not they're Christian, most, if not all, would probably say "yes." In fact, there's a good chance that some would look at you like you had two heads and say something clever, like "Does that building behind me look like a Jewish temple to you? Of course I'm Christian. What a stupid question!" Anyone who said that, though, wouldn't be telling you what he is. He'd be telling you what he *isn't*. He *isn't* Muslim, Jewish, Buddhist, etc. Therefore, in his mind, it must logically follow that he is Christian.

A Christian is someone who has surrendered his or her life to the sovereignty of Jesus Christ, and it is not evident by outward appearances. To know

27

for sure whether or not someone is a Christian, you would have to be able to see into the heart, and only God can do that. Simply attending the church of a particular denomination *does not* make someone a "Christian." Anyone who thinks it does must then also believe it is possible to become a U.S. Marine by going into a military surplus store and buying the right color uniform. It doesn't work that way. For the remainder of this book, whenever I use the term "Christian," I will be referring to someone who has given his or her life to Jesus Christ and, as a result, has been "born-again."

Frankly, I would not have recognized the fact that we Christians speak a unique language, were it not for an email conversation I had with a good friend on this very subject. She asked me whether or not Catholics are Christians. That question highlights my point perfectly. My answer was, "Not necessarily. It depends." The teaching of the Catholic Church is, in fact, guided by the fundamental tenets of Christianity, which are:

1. Jesus Christ was and is God (see John 1:1, 1:14 and Colossians 2:9).
2. He rose from the dead (see Matthew 28).
3. Salvation is by grace alone and cannot be earned (see Ephesians 2:8,9).

Any religious organization that teaches something contrary to those principles is not Christian. But my friend wasn't asking about an organization.

She wanted to know about the people. That's why I couldn't answer it.

The entire population of the Earth can be divided up into two groups: those who are "saved" and those who are "not saved." Which group each person belongs to doesn't have anything to do with whether he or she is Catholic, Protestant, non-denominational or whatever. It has *everything* to do with whether or not a conscious decision has been made to put Jesus Christ onto the throne of one's life. In fact, I believe one feature of Jesus' crucifixion was engineered in order to speak to this very issue. You may recall the scene as depicted in Luke 23:32-43. In that description, Jesus is hanging on the cross between two thieves. As you may know, they are often referred to as the good thief and the bad thief. The bad thief verbally abuses Jesus and chides him to get down off the cross and save himself. Then the good thief basically tells the bad one to knock it off. He says (paraphrasing), "We deserve to be here, but this man (Jesus) did nothing. Jesus, please remember me." Jesus then replies by saying, "Today you will be with me in paradise."

So what's significant about that? Although we're not told anything about the lives these thieves lived, it's probably pretty safe to assume that they neither attended "church" nor were baptized. However, with the simple surrender of his heart, the good thief secured a place for himself at Jesus' side in paradise. In the last moments of his life, he was "saved." I see that as a very clever representation of all of humankind.

Jesus wants to be the center figure in everyone's life. He hangs in the midst of all of us and we have to pick a side. Are we going to acknowledge Him or not? It's not a terribly complicated issue. Another scriptural passage, Matthew 25:31-46 paints a different "sight picture" that delivers the exact same message.

Before we delve into the nuts and bolts of what it takes to pick a side, we're going to have a look at the fate that awaits those who remain on the side of the bad thief. Our Lord does not beat around the bush on this subject. John 3:3 says, "In reply Jesus declared, 'I tell you the truth, no one can see the kingdom of God unless he is born again.'" Matthew 19:21-24, is a good companion to that scriptural passage. It is Jesus' response to a rich man who asks about getting into Heaven. It says, "Jesus answered, 'If you want to be perfect, go, sell your possessions and give to the poor, and you will have treasure in heaven. Then come, follow me.' When the young man heard this, he went away sad, because he had great wealth. Then Jesus said to his disciples, 'I tell you the truth, it is hard for a rich man to enter the kingdom of heaven. Again I tell you, it is easier for a camel to go through the eye of a needle than for a rich man to enter the kingdom of God!'"

A word of clarification is warranted here. Many passages in the Bible paint a very vivid sight picture but were not necessarily meant to be taken literally. If, for example, you happen to be enjoying a life filled with nice material things, I sincerely doubt God is asking you to get rid of them and devote yourself to a religious life that features poverty as one of its cornerstones. I do, however, think He is instructing all of us to be mindful of a trap into which we can easily fall. If money, in this example, is more important to you than Jesus Christ, then it (your money) and not He (Jesus) is the Lord of your life. That's exactly what He's telling us to avoid. Be aware of who (or what) your Lord really is and be honest with yourself in coming up with that answer. Waiting to figure that out until after an airplane hits your place of employment may be cutting it a bit too close.

A logical follow-up to that caution deserves our attention as well. On the surface, submitting to Jesus Christ's sovereignty may appear to consist of more pain than gain. While digesting everything Jesus has to say about how we should live our lives, you may be tempted to look for anything you can that would torpedo His message and justify the lifestyle to which you've become accustomed. Please don't use subtle differences in biblical passages to advance that effort. This book will, like most others written on this subject, contain various verses from the Bible. Different versions of the Bible use slightly different words all the time. For example, depending upon which version of the Bible you're using, the passage from John 3:3 that I cited above may use "born anew" or "born from above" in place of "born again." Don't use that fact to say, "well my Bible says 'born anew' so this 'born again' fanatic obviously isn't talking to me." First of all, you're right. *I'm* not talking to you. *The Lord of the universe is!* I'm just the mouthpiece.

31

Secondly, don't get so focused on the words that you miss the message. If you're concerned about the reliability of the Bible, don't be. It is beyond question. For more insight into this notion, I highly recommend Lee Strobel's outstanding work *The Case for Christ* or Dr. Don Bierle's *Surprised by Faith*. Both authors do a fantastic job of putting any questions as to the Bible's authenticity to rest once and for all.

One last disclaimer is worth mentioning. I've had some very compelling experiences in my life as an officer in the U.S. Air Force and as a pilot for United Airlines. As far as theology is concerned, though, I'm just one more face in the crowd. I have a Bachelor of Experience degree from the Shoe Leather Seminary—nothing more and nothing less. If I seem to *pontificate* from what appears to be a seat of great, enlightened authority, put that notion to rest right away! That's not my intent. I'm not writing this in order to indict anybody or scream, "You should be more like me." In fact, a true recipe for success would probably exist if you analyzed most of the decisions I've made in my life and then worked as hard as you could to do the exact opposite. My list of mistakes is long and impressive. The only difference that may exist between you and me is that I've already accepted Jesus' death on the cross as payment in full for those mistakes. The peace, joy and strength I've come to know as a result of that action is something I'd like you to experience as well. It certainly came in handy on 9/11!

CHAPTER THREE

Hell

We've already seen a case in scripture where the choice was clear-cut. Good thief or bad thief? Heaven or Hell? For the time being, let's abandon any notion of enticing ourselves with a vision of Heaven and focus, instead, on understanding the *only* other choice that awaits us when we leave this earth, namely, Hell!

Hollywood has done a pretty good job of reinforcing a commonly held view that Hell is a place including, among other things, fire. In fact, numerous passages in the Bible talk about Hell being a place where there is fire. We typically think of some evil looking humanoid form named Satan who is being tended to by a throng of minions with pointed ears and pitchforks. We sometimes also picture him enjoying a sinister laugh at the expense of the people who are consigned to his realm for eternity. As bad a mental image as that is for me, I actually think Hell is characterized by something so much worse that it defies description and really needs concentrated imagination to understand.

One of the great gifts God gave me was a boss at United Airlines who is a truly spirit-filled Christian. He shared his vision of Hell with me one day and it really struck a chord. It begins with an understanding of what we have here on earth. Ever since Jesus Christ rose from the grave and sent the Holy Spirit to dwell among us as our companion and guide, there has *never* existed a time for *anyone* on earth wherein a connection to God was not possible. Let me repeat that for emphasis. Nobody, no matter how sinful or destructive a lifestyle he or she has pursued, has ever been cut off from the *possibility* of turning away from that lifestyle and finding his or her way back home to Jesus and eternal salvation. No matter how dark and foreboding one's circumstances have been, there has *always* been the hope of a better day ahead and the potential of grasping it by giving all the pain and misery over to Jesus. Hell is a place where that possibility ceases to exist.

Truly try to imagine that! Close your eyes and give yourself over to that image. I don't see Hell so much as a place that's lit up by fire, as one where there is utter black hopelessness which fuels a gut-burning fire raging *inside* the eternal body of every occupant. It's almost too overwhelming to imagine for more than a passing moment. Picture an existence totally cut off from God and, hence, hope. Every instant of one's eternal life will be more terrifying than the one that preceded it. And that descent into progressively worsening horror *will never end.* No matter how hard one tries to muster up the assets needed to endure that existence by looking forward to a better day, I believe inhabitants of Hell will somehow know that a better day can never come to exist and that tomorrow will be even worse than today was. I know that when I'm struggling with a particularly daunting issue in my life, part of my coping mechanism is the knowledge that, someday, things will be better. I don't believe that will ever be true in Hell. Regardless of what Hell ultimately does "look like," I think most people would agree that it's a place to which we do not want to go.

At the beginning of this chapter, I mentioned something about the *only* choice we have while we're here on Earth. I truly believe, with all my heart, that there are no second chances after we die. Over the years I've tried to share the good news of the Gospel with numerous non-believers. A common question that I'm asked to address has to do with all the people who either lived prior to Jesus' birth, or came after Him, but died having never heard His name. "What about those folks?" they ask. "Are they consigned to eternity in Hell? That just doesn't pass the common sense test!" The answer I like to give to that question is, "I don't have the slightest idea how God intends to reveal Himself to people who fit that description, but I know exactly how He intends to reveal Himself to you. He made it possible for us to have this conversation."

I think it's important to admit to oneself why the question is asked in the first place. If one were to be honest, the real reason for asking that question lies in the hope that there's some sort of cosmic, heavenly second chance woven into the fabric of the universe. It would ideally be a second chance that makes it possible to defer the decision to give one's life over to Jesus Christ until more concrete information is available as to whether or not that's necessary.

Do yourself a favor and forget about that possibility because it doesn't exist. While there may be a lot of "off the beaten path" cults which believe that, they do not get their understanding from scripture. In fact, the Bible tells us the *exact opposite*. Hebrews 9:27-28 says, "Just as man is destined to die once, and after that to face judgment, so Christ was sacrificed once to take away the sins of many people; and he will appear a second time, not to bear sin, but to bring salvation to those who are waiting for him." That sounds pretty straightforward to me, and there are no second chances in that message! By the way, there is one more thought I want you to consider. If you are reading these words or have been introduced to Jesus Christ via some other means, the opportunity to choose has been put on the table. If there *is* a second chance for all the people who were never introduced to Jesus Christ while they were alive, that population does not include you. You've been made aware of the opportunity (and requirement) to choose. Also, keep in mind that doing nothing constitutes a course of action. If you delay your decision until after you die, you will have picked a side!

CHAPTER FOUR

Human
Colored Glasses

Now that we've had a look at what Hell might consist of, we know what it is from which we need to be "saved." But why do we need to worry about all of this "salvation by grace through faith in Jesus Christ" stuff in the first place? After all, aren't the majority of us decent, hard working people who mind their own business and, *more or less*, obey the Ten Commandments? Actually, the answer to that question is probably "yes." But is that good enough?! Scripture says "no." Romans 3:23 says, "for all have sinned and fall short of the glory of God." Notice that it doesn't say, "For the people who commit sins that other people think are really, really bad fall short of the glory of God." It says "all." The good news flip side to that message is that the only sin God *won't* forgive is *rejecting* Jesus Christ as your personal Lord and Savior. Saying, "thanks but no thanks" to that offer lines us up right behind the bad thief. That is the only sin God won't forgive.

Many books that look at this whole idea of salvation go into a history of the term "sin." They tell you it's actually a word with origins in the sport of archery and means, "missing the mark." Many years ago, apparently that was the word one would hear shouted out if the archer in a competition missed the bulls-eye on the target. As sinners, we certainly do "miss the bulls-eye" on a very routine basis, hence the connection. A very dear friend of mine, author Randy Newman (*Questioning Evangelism*, Kregel Publications, February 1, 2004) balked at the notion of including that history in this work when I asked for his editorial input. He said that however accurately it may seem to portray the problem, it actually *trivializes* it. One could listen to the history of the term "sin" and mistakenly believe that *some* of us are actually capable of overcoming our sinful nature because every once in a while, the archer actually *does* hit the bulls-eye. I'd never really thought of it that way, but he's absolutely right, and *that* is the point that I thought made the archery metaphor one worth including. If we want to adequately characterize sin and the absolute impossibility of defeating it by the fruits of our own effort, we'd have to put the target somewhere on Jupiter and *still* hit the bulls-eye. Only one individual in the history of humankind could ever do something like that, and His name is Jesus. Accepting His free offer of salvation amounts to nothing more than saying "yes," when He asks whether or not we want Him to shoot the arrow for us. It's that simple.

Let's take a quick look at why we fall into that trap of insisting that we shoot the arrow for ourselves. Sin, as seen through human colored glasses, comes in varying degrees of seriousness. For example, it's pretty unlikely that we'll ever read a headline from a newspaper that screams "Accused Jaywalker Found Guilty, Sentenced To Die By Lethal Injection." To us, there is a huge difference between double parking and double murder. That's what makes things so confusing. We're lulled, by our very own human nature, into thinking that we might actually be good enough on our own to deserve eternal life in Heaven. While we're told in various places throughout scripture that there are, in fact, varying "degrees" of sin, the bottom line for our purposes is that sin is sin—period. And, with the exception of Jesus Christ, every human is guilty of it the instant he or she is born. We have Adam and Eve to thank for that. It was their disobedience that caused them (and, consequently, us) to be permanently separated from God. That whole notion is wrapped up in the term *original sin*. From the moment we are born, we owe a bill that is due and payable. The good news is that Jesus Christ picked up the tab already and we're told that in Romans 5:8. "But God demonstrates his own love for us in this: While we were still sinners, Christ died for us."

To provide a human illustration, imagine your son coming home after a full day of playing with his friends. His shoes are caked with mud and he wants to come into your (more or less) nice, clean house. I don't know about your house, but in ours, *he's* allowed inside, but the dirty shoes are not. Heaven is God's house and the mud (sin) that's caking up our lives is not welcome there. It doesn't matter whether it was the little white lie you told when you insisted that the dog ate your homework or the murder you committed in order to eliminate your business competition. It's all sin, and there is no place for it in the sinless destination called Heaven. It doesn't matter if the shoes are caked with a little mud or a lot. They'll still get the carpet dirty and, consequently, will not be allowed in the house. *We* are allowed in, but the dirt has to be washed away first. When Christ died on the cross, his blood did that for us.

CHAPTER FIVE

Who's In Charge Around Here?!

In response to the reality that we're all wearing dirty shoes and can't get into God's house in that condition, what do we generally try to do about it? Frankly, we trip over our human nature in a futile attempt to take matters into our own hands. We live in what I like to call a transactional community. Our gut instinct says, "I do for you...you do for me." That very mindset is what leads many people to believe that if they just attend church faithfully every Sunday, donate money, and do nice things for people, God will recognize that and weigh it against all of our sins. As long as the scales tip the right way, we're in. Wrong! Please pay close attention to this next sentence. *You can't earn your way into Heaven...period!*

There is an important scriptural passage that speaks to this issue. Ephesians 2:8,9 says, "For it is by grace you have been saved, through faith-and this is not from yourselves, it is the gift of God—not by works, so that no one can boast." In other words, the price has been paid. It's a gift and it's available to every one of us. We can't do anything to earn it. Gifts have one very interesting feature, though. They're not officially gifts until they're *accepted.* Frankly, that fact thrills me, because if it were up to me to right the wrong of original sin through the work of my own hands, the story would have a very unhappy ending.

All of this boils down to a simple decision. We can either accept His gift of salvation by subordinating our lives to His Lordship or stubbornly refuse to do so. The most important word in that preceding sentence, by the way, is "subordinating." It represents the one pivotal mindset that must come to exist before anyone can fully understand what it means to accept Jesus Christ as his or her personal Lord and Savior and, hence, become a Christian. The term "subordinate" means to be subject to the authority or control of another. Matthew 19:30 says it a little differently. "But many who are first will be last, and many who are last will be first." Unfortunately, it's not part of our human nature to voluntarily make ourselves last, and that's where so many people fall eighteen inches short of salvation. The concept is in the brain, but it just doesn't make it down into the heart. Actually, there's a reason for that.

When talking about every instant of one's entire life on Earth, the thought of subordinating it to someone else's will and control is a tough pill to swallow. Let's not kid each other. Assuming a normal life span of seventy plus years, that's a very long time to "endure the effects of that decision!" Besides, like we just said, inborn human pride doesn't exactly lend itself to putting others first. When was the last time, for example, that you saw a two-year old blissfully give away his or her favorite toy just to keep a playmate happy? We're born with a "look out for number one" mindset. By the way, I believe the natural tendency to maintain control of our surroundings is a gift from God. He knew we would need it in order to survive. For example, all the way back in time when cavemen roamed the earth, they learned right away that they had to control the environment in which they hunted. In other words, they could either kill lunch, or *be* lunch. Now that strikes me as a pretty good reason to maintain control of one's surroundings! Choosing to give up *overall* control of our lives, however, is exactly what He wants us to do, no matter how counterintuitive it may feel to do so.

That fact gives rise to a very compelling question. Why did He create us with an inborn predisposition to do "X," only to then turn around and insist that we do "Y" in order to avoid eternity in Hell? That doesn't exactly fit my description of a loving, merciful God. In order to explore that question, we have to go beneath the surface and understand His intent, at least to the extent that He gives us the ability to do so. Before I do that, though, I'll cut right to the chase and tell you why. It's because He wants to *know* that our love for Him is *genuine*. He creates in us both the ability and requirement to choose!

It is called free will. Make no mistake. Brilliant thinkers throughout time have wrestled with that notion. For example, hundreds of years before Jesus was born, it was prophesied (Psalm 41:9) that one of His disciples would betray Him, and that's exactly what happened! But then how could it be said that that disciple (Judas Iscariot) was *free to choose* whether or not to do that? My answer to that daunting question is elegant in its simplicity: I don't have the slightest idea. Nor, frankly, do I care. Like so many other things in my relationship with my Savior, I'm just going to take it on faith that that's the way it is.

Be that as it may, let me try to highlight my point with an illustration. Pretend, for the sake of argument, that you have a five-year-old son. Sadly, you've been abusive and unloving to this child over the course of his life. Furthermore, you're keenly aware of appearances, so you've threatened your son with more abuse if he doesn't proclaim in a loud voice, "I love you, Daddy!" whenever he's within earshot of witnesses. Now here's the big question. Do those witnesses think he loves you? Probably. Does he really? I doubt it! If given the actual right to freely choose whether or not to say, "I love you Daddy," what do you think he'd say? I know what I think, but this book is supposed to be G-rated so I'm not going to print it here. You get my point, though. If God either compelled or pre-wired us to say or do "X," it wouldn't be genuine. I would never presume to put words into my Lord's mouth, but I'd be willing to bet that He wants our love for Him to be genuine. In other words, He wants it to be our idea to love Him! Also, once we make our free choice to do that, we will have fulfilled the reason He created all of us, in the first place, to have fellowship with Him!

In my view, there's actually one other reason He's made this whole dynamic somewhat confusing. I think He intentionally made it impossible for us to completely and thoroughly know him, before *or* after we choose him, because He wants our love relationship with Him to be an active, 24/7 thing. He wants us to continue to seek him, day in and day out. Again, an illustration might help. If you lose something, you look for it. If you find it, do you keep looking for it? Of course not. You put it back where it belongs and, in all likelihood, forget about it until the next time you need it. That whole "forget about it (Him) until the next time you need it (Him)" thing is precisely what He *doesn't* want our relationship with Him to be. Therefore, He makes it necessary for us to explicitly and deliberately choose Him and then spend the rest of our lives *seeking* Him, twenty-four hours per day, in an attempt to get to know Him. Don't kid yourself. The ride won't be without bumps, but oh, what a destination!!

Now that we understand why it's necessary to explicitly choose Him and then spend the rest of our lives seeking Him, let's return to that "I do for you...you do for me" mindset with which we're all pre-wired at birth. Forget (at least for now) everything else the Bible tells us about how to live our lives. Let's just focus on the standard we need to satisfy in order to be acceptable to God *without* an intermediary (His son, Jesus Christ). That standard is called the Ten Commandments. Here's where the notion that we're good enough for Heaven breaks down. At the risk of making judgments about what would and would not be easy for any one particular individual, I see some of the Commandments as "no-brainers." For the sake of illustration, let's take them in order.

1. "You shall have no other gods before me." No problem.
2. "You shall not make for yourself an idol..." Again, no problem.
3. "You shall not misuse the name of the Lord your God..." Don't swear?! I get this one *mostly* right. (OK, there's a little mud on those shoes, now).
4. "Remember the Sabbath day by keeping it holy." Did you ever wake up on Sunday and just blow off church because you didn't feel like getting out of bed?
5. "Honor your father and your mother..." Well, I think I do this one pretty well.
6. "You shall not murder." No problem...wasn't planning to anyway!

7. "You shall not commit adultery." I actually thought I was in pretty good shape on this one until I read Matthew 5:28, "But I tell you that anyone who looks at a woman lustfully has already committed adultery with her in his heart." In other words, no clothes have to come off. God sees the content of your heart!

8. "You shall not steal." Again, at first glance, most of us would probably think we're OK with this one. But, have you ever called in sick to your job when you weren't really sick? Have you ever known that you were given too much change by a cashier and didn't bring it to his or her attention? Did you ever claim that your thirteen year-old child was twelve so you could order from the cheaper child's menu? The list goes on, but it's all ill-gotten gain—it's stealing.

9. "You shall not give false testimony against your neighbor." In other words, don't lie. Oops! Just called in sick and actually feel fine. Two birds with one stone?

10. "You shall not covet your neighbor's house." Uh huh… Don't you ever see something someone else has, and want it for yourself? Again, oops.

I came out of this exercise with Commandments 1, 2, 5, and 6 in pretty good shape. The other six are just mud on my shoes. The important thing for me to remember is that I think I'm a pretty decent guy and, compared to a serial murderer, I guess I am. But that serial murderer isn't the standard against which I am to be judged. The standard is perfection, because that's what is awaiting us in God's house. Based on that standard, at one time or another in my life, I've been a lying, swearing, stealing adulterer whose church attendance record on the Sabbath is less than spotless.

What we're really talking about here is the work of human hands. I don't care how many good deeds you're performing or how hard you're trying to live a life that you think will please God. If you haven't invited Him into a personal, one-on-one active relationship while in this *very* temporary housing situation we call "Earth," you're going to wind up on judgment day with mud on your shoes.

On the subject of works, rest assured that they have a very prominent role to play in this dynamic *after* you make Jesus the Lord of your life. James 2:17 says, "In the same way, faith by itself, if it is not accompanied by action, is dead." The key thing to remember, though, is that you've got to get them in the right order. No faith, and a lifetime of works, equals no *eternal* significance. Conversely, faith with no works, we're told, is "dead." Faith and true subordination of one's will to the will of Jesus leads to a lifetime of works that *He* will inspire you to complete.

CHAPTER SIX

Affairs Of The Heart

As you may have been able to glean thus far, there is a rather important fundamental difference between the way we see the world and the way God sees it. Basically, our senses perceive what they perceive. God, however, can see things we can't. He can see through to our hearts. That's important because that's where all the action that matters to Him takes place. Incidentally, that's also why you can't pull the wool over His eyes. Your attempts to *appear* to care about His kingdom by faithfully attending church, but then sitting there wondering what time the ballgame starts, will amount to nothing. He knows! Perhaps a few "sight pictures" will clear up what I'm trying to say about focusing on the content of one's heart.

Pretend, for the sake of illustration, that you witness the following event. You're standing a few feet behind a park bench on a beautiful day. On one end of this short bench, there sits a young African-American woman who is minding her own business and simply enjoying the peaceful setting. Along comes a young white woman with her precocious three-year old daughter and their golden retriever puppy. The little girl is the picture of sweet innocence. She's a blond haired, blue-eyed cutie with a big smile and a brand new, brightly colored sundress. They, too, are simply out to enjoy the weather, play with the dog and swing on the swings. Before they do all that, though, mom decides to take a break and sits down on the other end of the same park bench. By the way, any of you who have ever been the parent of a three-year old probably know by now that the "sit and take a break" part of the plan will most likely not include the three-year old. They are generally not programmed to sit still for very long, if at all. As Mom does manage to catch a few minutes of peace and quiet, the girl happily skips down to the black lady and says, "Hi!" The lady smiles and cheerfully says "Hi!" right back. Then the little girl, as only three-year olds can, lifts the front of her dress up to her chin and proudly proclaims, "Mommy bought me brand new Sesame Street underwear! Do you like it?!!" The lady does her best to keep a straight face, throws a sidelong wink at Mom, and says, "Wow…that's the prettiest underwear I've seen all day!" The little girl then excitedly runs back to Mom with her hands covering her mouth, jumps up and down a few times, and then says in a loud voice (much to Mom's embarrassment and dismay), "Mommy!! That chocolate lady says I have pretty underwear! Can I go swing on the swings?!" Mom drops her head to her chest and shakes it ruefully while quietly wondering whether or not it's possible to completely disappear from view by hiding behind a puppy-sized golden retriever.

Now for the big question. If this were a real encounter, would you expect the young black woman to be horribly offended by the "racial slur" that just flew in her direction? I seriously doubt it. Why not? Because we know that it wasn't meant to be a racial slur! The little girl's words (at least the way an *adult* might interpret them) did not communicate what was in her heart, and somehow we all just intuitively know that. She was just thrilled that someone liked her underwear, wanted to share that great news, and did so by expressing herself in the only way she knew how. There's nothing but innocent love in that entire scenario. We, as adults, slowly learn how to conceal what's in our hearts from one another, but kids don't know how to do that. They haven't been polluted by the sin of the world yet, and still enjoy that enviable state of uncorrupted ignorance. Sometimes I wonder whether it is adults or children who are truly ignorant.

Perhaps all of this is what our Lord was driving at in Matthew 18:1-6:

"At that time the disciples came to Jesus and asked, 'Who is the greatest in the kingdom of

52

heaven?' He called a little child and had him stand among them. And he said: 'I tell you the truth, unless you change and become like little children, you will never enter the kingdom of heaven. Therefore, whoever humbles himself like this child, is the greatest in the kingdom of heaven. And whoever welcomes a little child like this in my name welcomes me. But if anyone causes one of these little ones who believe in me to sin, it would be better for him to have a large millstone hung around his neck and to be drowned in the depth of the sea.'"

Incidentally, if you're silently applauding my vivid imagination for coming up with that park bench scenario I just described, don't waste your energy. My wife and I have two kids who are both older than three. That incident wouldn't even win honorable mention in the battle of wits we've fought (and occasionally lost) over the years!

Another actual encounter in my own life showed me just exactly what is meant by the need to focus on the content of one's heart. All the way back in the mid-1980's, I met and eventually married my wife, Susan. As odd as this may sound, though, I can't tell you the exact date when we married. I can only tell you when the ceremony took place. In the interest of setting the stage for this life lesson, it is worth it for you to know that my wife and I met on a blind date when I was visiting Washington D.C. in April 1984. At that time, I was based in Mississippi in the Air Force and my future bride lived in Northern Virginia. From the day we met until the day we walked down the aisle together, we lived 1000 miles apart. I'm pretty sure the Bell Telephone Company shareholder's meeting was a happy event that year. Shortly after proposing to Susan, I was back down at work in Mississippi. One afternoon in the chow hall, I happened to make what I thought was an innocent comment to a co-worker. I mentioned that I thought one of the young ladies working in the serving line was attractive. He said, "You ought to ask her out." I reminded him that I'd just gotten engaged. His response to that was, "Yeah, but you're not married yet. You're a free agent up until the day you say 'I do.'"

Now in all likelihood, some of you are saying, "Yeah, right on!" (Probably mostly guys). The rest of you are saying, "What a pig!" Whatever your opinion may be, the important point is that in my mind, I was actually already married. In fact, I became emotionally, mentally and spiritually married to Susan at the exact instant when I sat in my apartment in Mississippi, all by myself, and decided to ask her to marry me. That's why I can't tell you when we actually got married. I don't remember what the exact date was when I did that. But until and unless she said "no," I was off the market. Society, as we know it today, has worked very hard to relegate ideas like that to the dark recesses of our consciousness. They *never* escape God's field of vision, though. He sees the content of our hearts!

Speaking of darkness and the content of our hearts, I often hear one other objection to the notion of surrendering one's life to the Lordship of Jesus Christ. Those same skeptics who hope for second chances after death sometimes cite evil as a reason to insist that God doesn't even exist, let alone that we need to voluntarily give our lives to His Son. They often say something like, "Why would an all-loving God create evil? Since there is such a thing as evil, there must not be an all-loving God." My answer, again, is somewhat elegant in its simplicity. God didn't actually create evil, because evil isn't a "something." It is the *absence* of a something. Namely, it's the absence of good. God is "good." We humans chose to reject Him, and evil is what has come to pass as a result.

It might be a little bit easier to grasp this idea by equating it to something with which we are more familiar—namely darkness and light—especially in view of the fact that "light" is one of the names by which we've come to know Jesus. John 8:12 says, "When Jesus spoke again to the people, he said, 'I am the light of the world.'"

Believe it or not, it's actually impossible to *measure* darkness. One can only measure light. In a totally pitch-black room, for example, one wouldn't say there's a whole bunch of darkness. There just isn't any light. In a *pretty* dark room, you wouldn't say there's a little *less darkness* than there was in the pitch-black room. You'd say there is a little more light.

The point worth considering is that God didn't create evil. Man exercised his free will and chose to separate himself from God in the Garden of Eden. It wasn't until then that goodness was able to be absent from our lives. We've been coping with that unfortunate fact ever since. The irony in all of this is that the absence of good actually answers our skeptics' objection. The fact that we can recognize that there is an ultimate standard we call "good" proves that there is an infinitely loving God. If that weren't the case, we wouldn't recognize any difference between good "stuff" and evil "stuff." There would just be ... "stuff." This also ties back perfectly to our discussion on the Ten Commandments and the fallacy that we are good enough on our own to merit the rewards in Heaven. Our thinking is the exact opposite of what it should be. We think we ought to get high fives and pats on the back *if we just don't violate all Ten*. In reality, though, our only hope of ever seeing Heaven is tied to Jesus Christ *if we don't perfectly comply with all Ten on our own*. By the way, it's impossible to do that! Matthew 19:25-26 says, "When the disciples heard this they were greatly astonished and asked, 'Who then can be saved?' Jesus looked at them and said, 'With man this is impossible, but with God all things are possible.'"

There's one other interesting facet of this issue that deserves our attention. We already established that there is a God, because we can recognize the difference between good and evil. That reality exists today because God *allowed us to reject Him!* So,

56

if He didn't rescind the gift of free will in order to prevent us from making the worst possible choice we could have, why would He rescind it now and make it impossible to undo the damage? Leaving our ability to choose Him intact is probably one of the most compelling acts of mercy He's ever performed on our behalf. He made it possible to re-connect. He's also given us an outward and visible manifestation of Himself so that we will know *through whom* to re-connect (Jesus Christ) and *how* to re-connect (exercise our free will). The *only* piece of the puzzle that He's left for us to fit into place is *when*. In my mind's eye, "right now" looks like a pretty good option! I think a lot of my colleagues in the Pentagon thought so as well on September 11, when the smell of smoke began to permeate the atmosphere. None of us knows when our last chance to choose Him will have come and gone. Matthew 24:44, puts it quite succinctly. "So you also must be ready, because the Son of Man will come at an hour when you do not expect him."

CHAPTER SEVEN

What Now?

If you recall, at the beginning of this discussion I said that, in a sense, you were reading a sales brochure. Continuing with that analogy, the one piece of this transaction that is still on the table is the "close." As soon as you are ready to make that choice for our Lord, a simple prayer of salvation appears at the end of this book. I can't tell you how much I hope you go there right now and pray it! Once you do that, you will be "saved." However, your journey will have only just begun.

Once you pray the prayer of salvation, what's going to happen? That's the question I posed as the title for this book. If you accept Jesus Christ as your personal Lord and Savior and become a new creation, will something outward and visible suddenly happen? Will the skies part and the heavenly host fill your field of vision? Will thunder rain down from on high? Will your face glow like Moses' did? (See Exodus 34:33-35.) Frankly, I doubt it. Don't be fooled, though. Something miraculous and heavenly will definitely have come to pass, instantaneously. The Holy Spirit will have taken up residence in your heart! As a consequence of that fact, the "old" you will have ceased to exist and a "new" you will have been created. Hence the term "born again" or "re-born" or whatever you want to call it. My personal preference is to say I'm "saved" because I no longer have to fear the horrors of hell!

Since we've listed a few things that probably *won't* happen when you give your life to the Lord, what *will* happen? You will begin to grow! For example, certain behavior will *eventually* no longer appeal to you, but it probably won't disappear overnight. I remember a conversation I had one time with a wonderful Christian lady. She told me about a man whom she'd led to Christ. Two weeks later, this same man called up very upset. He said that he'd given into temptation, done something he shouldn't have, and was now afraid that he was no longer a Christian. The following dialogue took place.

Friend:	"Does your behavior bother you?"
Man:	"Of course!"
Friend:	"Would that behavior have bothered you before you accepted Christ?"
Man:	"No."
Friend:	"Sounds like you're a Christian to me!"

The important message is this. Christians don't stop being sinners. They stop being *condemned* sinners!

One other interesting dynamic will probably come into play for you, because it did for me, and has for a lot of my Christian friends as well. My behavior has changed over time because I just don't want to let down my friend Jesus. What I think, do and say is a direct reflection of Him. Jesus' parting words to us all those years ago were spelled out in Matthew 28:19. Jesus Himself says, "Therefore go and make disciples of all nations, baptizing them in the name of the Father and of the Son and of the Holy Spirit...." In this context, actions truly do speak louder than words. The "do as I say and not as I do" method of evangelism does not work well.

The bottom line is this. You change the instant you pray the prayer of salvation. When that happens, though, you become a work in progress. Newborn babies are capable of doing virtually nothing for themselves, but that doesn't make them any less human. Physical birth begins a process that consists of growth and development, among other things. So does Christian rebirth. Someone who has just become saved is a brand new creation who is just beginning an awesome journey of discovery. As I said, you don't stop being a sinner once you're born again. You stop being a *condemned* sinner. Also, the "good works" (church attendance, etc.) you thought you were pursuing to rack up those heavenly brownie points will just naturally begin to be part of your life, but for a different reason. God will have laid it on your heart and given you some idea of which "works" He wants you to complete. For example, you may find yourself more aware of the suffering around you that you never used to see. You may find yourself compelled to support a given charity because now their work matters to you. The point is that God will be leading you, instead of you trying to lead God. You will be an unending work in progress. But you'll be one of God's works in progress, and that's what counts. One of the best bumper stickers I've ever seen said, "Be patient...God's not through with me yet." Truer words were never spoken.

CHAPTER EIGHT

How Did It Begin For Me?

I n the pages that follow, I've shared a few episodes from my own life. The only purpose in doing so is to give you something to compare and contrast against the light of your own background, experience and values. The first experience that makes sense for me to share with you is the one wherein I took my own advice and began a personal relationship with Jesus Christ.

I became a Christian while attending Kenmore East Senior High School in Tonawanda, N.Y. A friend invited me out for coffee one day, and in the course of our visit, "witnessed" to me, introducing this whole idea of having a personal relationship with Jesus Christ. I did not accept the invitation right on the spot, but was skeptical and reluctant. As I recall, I even returned home and commented to my parents that my friend had gone over the edge, so to speak, and become a religious fanatic. Eventually, though, I found myself thinking about it at odd times of the day and night. I just couldn't shake off the conversation we'd had and later realized that what I was experiencing was Jesus' knocking on the door of my heart, asking to be let in. I got to the point where I could no longer ignore that "noise." I eventually realized that my friend really did know what she was talking about, so I took a leap of faith and prayed the prayer of salvation. I let Him in and, so far as I could tell, absolutely nothing happened! My first memory of anything truly "divine" occurring in my life as a result of asking Jesus to take control didn't come to pass until two years later.

As I mentioned in the very first chapter, I knew I wanted to be an airline pilot way back at the ripe old age of five. I remember my father taking me out to the airport near our home just to watch airplanes. As soon as I saw, felt and heard that very first jet takeoff, I looked up at him and said, "I want to be a pilot." From that day on, I never seriously entertained the thought of any other career. In my sophomore year of college, I decided that the Air Force ROTC (Reserve Officer Training Corps) program would be the avenue I'd travel in my quest to realize my dream. Unfortunately, the only way I could be guaranteed a pilot training slot would be if I successfully competed for an ROTC Pilot Scholarship.

This was all playing out in the mid-1970's. The military was in its post-Vietnam draw down era and pilots were a dime a dozen. Without a guaranteed slot in pilot training, I could still participate in ROTC, but the odds of getting selected to be a pilot were miniscule. The ROTC recruiter with whom I was working happened to look at my SAT (Scholastic Aptitude Test) scores and said they were too low to be competitive for a scholarship. When I asked him what I would need, he said, "1200 ought to do the trick." So, as a sophomore in college, I arranged to take the SAT's all over again. This was a particularly daunting challenge because I'd left all of that test-able material in the rear view mirror three years earlier!

We're not really supposed to "test" God because doing so shows a lack of faith. In a sense, though, I guess I did anyway. I was a (more or less) brand new Christian so I thought I'd see if God was really ready to keep His promise as provided for in Matthew 7:7: "Ask and it will be given you..." On the morning of the test, I prayed and asked God for a 1200 in Jesus' name. As I sat at the desk waiting for the proctor's order to begin, I even went as far as to ask Him to show me which of the two pencils I should use that were sitting there on my desk. Just as I did that, I inadvertently kicked a leg of the desk while shift-ing in my seat and one pencil rolled towards me. I remember thinking "Well, OK, I guess I should use that one!" After the test was over, I went back to my dorm room and was lying on my bed thinking things over. Without intending to, I suddenly sat up in bed and uttered the words "I got the 1200."

It was as involuntary an action as pulling my hand off of a hot stove would have been. I then got on my knees, claimed God's gift to me in Jesus' name and gave Him thanks.

Approximately six weeks later, my father called to tell me that my scores had come in the mail. My knees nearly buckled when he read them to me… Verbal 560, Math 640…total 1200!! Not 1199…not 1201…1200! I've claimed that as a direct miracle from God ever since. By the way, I got the scholarship, enrolled in ROTC at Bowling Green State University in Ohio and then went on to fly in the Air Force. After leaving active duty, my ultimate dream came true when I was invited to become a pilot for United Airlines. And then came September 11th!

CHAPTER NINE

Life In The Trenches

Shortly after going to work for United Airlines, I began an affiliation with an outstanding group of Christians collectively known as the Fellowship of Christian Airline Personnel (www.fcap.org). FCAP's membership consists of employees from companies that virtually span the globe. The group's charter is to recognize that the workplace is a ministry field where we ought to be working to spread the good news of the Gospel. That story needs to be told everywhere! In the course of trying to do my part, I've written a number of articles, some of which appeared in FCAP's newsletter called the Trim Tab.

Some of those articles appear below. They were obviously written for an audience that consisted of fellow airline industry employees. Those messages of hope were directed toward people whose jobs, pensions, and lives are literally melting out from under them. Those specific tragedies may not be relevant to your particular situation, but no life is without trials and tribulations. If these stories do nothing else, they'll reinforce the reality that living for Jesus Christ does not guarantee a worry free life. It just guarantees that you'll never face it alone. Meditate on Psalm 139:7-10:

> "Where can I go from your Spirit? Where can I flee from your presence? If I go up to the heavens, you are there; if I make my bed in the depths, you are there. If I rise on the wings of the dawn, if I settle on the far side of the sea, even there your hand will guide me, your right hand will hold me fast."

WORRY, STRESS, AND OTHER SPIRITUAL DISTRACTERS (WRITTEN 12/9/2002)

There's a better than average chance that the title of this essay led you to think I picked this topic in order to be able to minister to you as the challenges of day-to-day living continue their slow, relentless attack on your ability to "don't worry...be happy." Actually, that's only partially correct. I'm also writing about this topic in hopes of ministering *to me!* Even as we "speak," the date is December 9, 2002 and it is approximately 9:30 A.M., Eastern Standard Time. That date and time may not strike a chord for everyone, but they certainly do for me. I am a Captain for United Airlines. A few short hours ago, my employer declared bankruptcy.

Approximately twelve years ago, my wife Susan, five months pregnant with our first child (a son we named Logan) was home to receive the mail while I was at work as a fulltime pilot for the U.S. Air Force Reserve. A letter was in there from United Airlines informing me that I'd successfully navigated the interview obstacle course and was now invited to join the ranks of one of the world's premier airlines. Upon arriving home from work that day, I couldn't believe my eyes as I walked up the sidewalk leading to the front door of our townhouse in Woodbridge, Virginia. Just a few moments before, my uncertain future had me so preoccupied in thought that I'd driven right past it without noticing that she'd decorated it with balloons, streamers and a big sign announcing the news. It would be pointless to try and communicate the emotion of that moment as the sight of her loving efforts registered on my brain. In one beautiful, succinct display, she was announcing to me that the professional pursuit of my lifetime had been achieved! I vaguely remember a saying from several years ago that went something like "the future's so bright, I gotta wear shades." That's exactly how I felt. I was married to my best friend, our first child was on his way (after four heart-wrenching years of trying to get pregnant and beginning to wonder whether or not one of us was unable to have children), and I'd just been offered the only job I'd ever really wanted. No man had ever been more richly blessed. In light of the fact that my future is, once again, so uncertain, it may come as a surprise to hear me say that I still am blessed beyond all understanding, but for a very different reason.

The townhouse scene I just painted for you, I am confident, was a metaphor for something that's playing out in a lot of lives right now. The fact that I drove right past my own front door without seeing the decorations has me wondering what I (and thousands of my other airline brothers and sisters) might *not* be seeing right now. Make no mistake—these are frightening times. I wouldn't bet one dollar that I will be an airline pilot at this time next year. But I know I'll be doing something, because Jesus is alive in my heart and has a plan for me that will come to pass whether I know what it is or not. Matthew 6:34 says, "Therefore do not worry about tomorrow, for tomorrow will worry about itself. Each day has enough trouble of its own." Good advice…not always easy to take…but good advice! In the quiet moments of my life when I get to enjoy completely undistracted communion with my personal Lord and Savior, I sometimes find myself asking for Him to (yet again) tell me that everything is going to be OK. He's probably screaming at me right now, saying something like *"for crying out loud, Dale, you belong to Me! Trust Me! You're going to be fine. Remember that whole Matthew 6:25-30 thing about birds eating what they didn't plant and flowers appearing to be more beautifully adorned than Solomon? I meant that. Now relax already!"* Somehow, the thought of responding to that with "Oh yea? Well, You may have died on the cross but I have to make a mortgage payment!" strikes me as a bad idea.

So as I valiantly try to minister to myself, let's take a look at worry. In a recent fit of reckless consumerism, I treated myself to a copy of The Life Application Study Bible published by Tyndale House Publications, Inc. If you're looking for a good Bible, I highly recommend this one. On the page that provided me with the passages to which I just referred, some guidance is offered in the notes section. It's entitled "Seven Reasons Not To Worry." Those notes and the verses from Matthew to which they apply appear as follows:

- The same God who created life in you can be trusted with the details of your life. (Matt. 6:25)
- Worrying about the future hampers your efforts for today. (Matt. 6:26)
- Worrying is more harmful than helpful. (Matt. 6:27)
- God does not ignore those who depend on him. (Matt. 6:28-30)
- Worrying shows a lack of faith in and understanding of God. (Matt. 6:31,32)
- Worrying keeps us from real challenges God wants us to pursue. (Matt. 6:33)
- Living one day at a time keeps us from being consumed with worry. (Matt. 6:34)

All of those observations are certainly accurate and compelling, but as I thought them over in light of their role as a backdrop for my life, I began to be aware of an interesting notion. In a somewhat demented way, anxiety-producing events might actually be playing a beneficial role in my relationship to Jesus Christ. While looking back over my life, I've seen many such events amount to significantly less than my imagination led me to fear they would be. However, my gaze was unwaveringly riveted on Him the whole time. When times have been good, though, He has been conspicuously absent from my conscious thought processes until I've eventually remembered to include Him by saying something cerebral like "Oops...oh yeah...Thank you, Father, for

71

the good times too." Has anyone out there (besides me) ever prayed as follows? "Thank you, Father, for the food I am about to receive and the stuff already in my mouth." I'm obviously not proud of that, but I'd be lying if I said it never happens. Even after all these years as a Christian, I've got a long ways to go when it comes to properly worshipping my Lord. I guess knowing that is a step in the right direction, but I also know that I will virtually never be able to demonstrate my love for Him in a way that does not pale in comparison to His ability to do the same for me. He wants my gaze to be riveted on Him 24 hours per day, 7 days per week! If the only way He can make that happen is to make me especially inept in the business of letting "the day's trouble be sufficient for the day," then so be it! That will be a very small price to pay for the ultimate prize that I, like every other Christian, will inherit someday—eternal life in the presence of Christ!

DO UNTO OTHERS
(WRITTEN 8/27/2003)

Over the course of many years, I've come to the realization that I entered this world handicapped by a very annoying birth defect. I am incapable of mastering anything unless I am allowed to apply whatever it is I was just taught, and then hurt myself by doing it incorrectly at least once. Until I complete that process, I just can't claim that the learning objective in question has been achieved. Actually, that's probably not the most comforting thing you could possibly hear a commercial airline pilot say, but you can relax because people like me are why simulators were invented. Unfortunately, there's a critical behavior that God asks us to exhibit and it can't be duplicated in a simulator. It's called "go out and be light and salt to the world."

Right after September 11, I was fairly confident that I was doing a pretty good job of putting on a happy Christian face and giving others encouragement to fight the good fight. Little did I know, God was setting me up for one of those "go out and hurt yourself" learning experiences. Before too long, *my* airline (UAL) declared bankruptcy and I began living life under the shadow of increased work hours for way less pay, cancellation of our ESOP stock, possible loss of my house, and the list goes on. I was now experiencing all the things that recipients of my pep talks were living through and, for some strange reason, the medicine I was peddling didn't taste all that good. As a result of that realization, I found I was losing my energy for (and sensing the futility of) trying to be the light that would attract others to Christ. From time to time, we pilots have to execute instrument approaches through unusually bad weather. At the end of approach briefings on days like that, I sometimes jokingly comment that *anyone* can succeed under ideal conditions. I couldn't shake the notion that my witness for Jesus Christ wasn't particularly effective unless conditions were ideal. Now that I was the one who was hurting, albeit to a far lesser degree than many others in this industry, my true character was showing through and I didn't like what I saw. My situation falls squarely into what I like to refer to as "The Broken Leg Syndrome." Maybe some of you can relate.

Paint the following picture in your mind. You're lying in a hospital bed with your newly broken leg entombed in a plaster cast. As you're lying there, the door to your room swings open and your new roommate is wheeled in, having just come from surgery to relieve the pain caused by an incurable disease that will lead to his death within the next six months. The $64,000.00 question is this: does your broken leg still hurt? What a ridiculous question. Of course it does! Frankly, I've been wrestling with this question a lot lately.

I'm not particularly proud of the fact that I really want people to know that I'm hurting and that they should feel sorry for me.

Dale: "I've taken a huge cut in salary."

God: "But others in your industry have lost more."

Dale: "I've lost a lot of seniority."

God: "You still have a job."

Dale: "I don't see my loved ones as often as I'd like because I have to work more hours to earn less pay."

God: "You're loved ones are all still alive."

Dale: "When am I ever going to feel better about these things?"

God: "As soon as you learn to trust me and realize, once and for all, that your security is in my hands. I am all you need!

One of the things that led me to stop and really take stock of myself was the message embodied in The Golden Rule: "Do unto others, as you would have them do unto you." The "others" in this case are my fellow foot soldiers here in the airline industry, especially the folks who work on our Crew Desk, assigning open trips to us pilots who are too junior to hold a regular schedule of flying. After each encounter I have with them, as well as every other teammate I have in this ministry field we call a workplace, I've begun to ask myself whether my demeanor and tone of voice made their day better or worse. In the case of the crew schedulers, for example, they truly are just the messengers who get paid to deliver bad news, such as, "You only *thought* you had a day off tomorrow. You're the only pilot available at the crew base, and you have to work."

Every one of us probably has the image of some industry leader(s), either past or present, which we believe contributed most directly to conditions that now define our lives. Seeking revenge against them by taking it out on our fellow victims makes no sense whatsoever. In fact, seeking revenge in the first place flies directly in the face of unequivocal guidance our Lord gave us in the Bible. Romans 12:19 says, "Do not take revenge, my friends, but leave room for God's wrath, for it is written: 'It is mine to avenge; I will repay,' says the Lord." It might feel good, but it sure isn't what God had in mind!

The bottom line issue that I've really begun to try and remember is this. At the end of every encounter I have in this life, one of two things will be true. The light of Jesus Christ either will or will not have shined through me. One of my worst fears is that I've recently allowed my 'broken leg' to overshadow the mission that Jesus has given me to be light and salt to the world. During one of my dark moods recently, a friend of mine commented that I seemed pretty "down." I began to articulate all the reasons that everyone should feel sorry for me and that all of my "don't worry…be happy" rhetoric seemed pretty futile. She responded by saying "Yeah, Dale, you're right, but you just never know when a simple smile or a kind word might be the one thing someone needs to get through their day." Amen to that!

DON'T TRY TO BOIL THE OCEAN (WRITTEN 4/10/2004)

While surfing around the radio dial recently, I stumbled onto a "call-in" program on one of my favorite Christian radio stations. The hosts of the program were men of God, well qualified to comment on issues and give sound scriptural answers to callers' questions. The reason I like this particular program is that listeners often call in to ask questions that I wish I had the chance to ask. That alone is comforting because from time to time, I forget that I'm not the only dazed and confused guy out here trying to make sense of things. When I hear other folks call in to discuss daunting personal issues, I am reminded of the old adage "misery loves company."

Be that as it may, on this particular day a listener called in with a concern that I've harbored for quite sometime. She was lamenting the fact that humankind seems to be heading into the spiritual scrap heap and was trying to get a handle on what God wanted her to do about it. It seemed evident to me that this particular lady was sincerely in love with the Lord and felt a real call to get involved. She talked about organizing prayer events, engaging public servants in discourse, marshalling fellow believers into action, etc, etc. She just didn't know which activity she should pursue and wanted to know what the Bible had to say on the subject. It was almost as if the menu had too many choices and she didn't know which entrée to consume. Then I thought about me.

On any given day, I consider my life to have been *wildly* successful if the list of things I absolutely MUST do before my head hits the pillow only grows by one or two things before my head hits the pillow.

Typical personal checklist:

1. Pay bills – check
2. Take out garbage – check
3. Run to Walmart; buy supplies for daughter's school project due tomorrow, even though she's known about it for the last two weeks – check
4. Unload dishwasher – check
5. Feed Misty (guinea pig) – check
6. Prepare backup income stream in case airline job goes away – check
7. Play one-on-one basketball with son – check
8. Punish son for beating father at one-on-one basketball – check
9. Solve world hunger – check
10. Get the Supreme Court to allow prayer in public school – check

You get the idea. A day rarely goes by when I don't question whether or not I'm doing enough to fulfill Jesus' command to go out and make disciples of all nations. In the very next thought, though, I have to remind myself that God appointed me to be, first and foremost, the CEO of my household.

Every minute I spend actually trying to solve world hunger is another minute I can't spend leading my children into a deeper and more meaningful personal relationship with their Lord and Savior, Jesus Christ. And, given the odds against my successfully solving world hunger, I'd be willing to bet that I can make a bigger impact on society by helping two wide-eyed children become two God-fearing adults with hearts for doing His will in their lives.

All of that does give rise to a question that deserves some attention, though. Since I can't be in the presence of my wife and kids 24/7, what should I do for my Lord when I'm otherwise occupied? That's easy! Saint Francis of Assisi hit that nail on the head when he said, "Preach Jesus and, if you must, use words." Have you ever been hustling through an airport terminal, only to come upon a confused looking passenger who obviously doesn't have the slightest idea where he needs to go next? If you take the thirty seconds that will be required to ask him if he needs help without waiting for him to ask you first, you will have shown him Jesus! When was the last time you were headed into a grocery store and saw a young mother trying to push a stroller with one hand AND pull a shopping cart full of food to her car with the other? If you ever see that and decide to put off your shopping trip for five minutes so that you can push her cart to the car for her, you will have done as it says to do in Matthew 25:40. "The King will reply, 'I tell you the truth, whatever you did for one of the least of these brothers of mine, you did for me.'"

Will world hunger ever get solved in my lifetime? Probably not. Will the hungry person that the Lord points out to me today get a sandwich? You bet! By the way, you may be asking yourself how I've got time to sit down and write this article if I'm so preoccupied with the tasks of life. Yet again, I woke up at 04:00 this morning, trying to decide how to bring peace to the Middle East. Since getting back to sleep was clearly not going to be an option, I decided to get up and write. Besides, before I went to bed last night, I pre-packed my two kids' school lunches and threw a fist full of lettuce into Misty's cage. That ought to keep all three of them from squawking at me for at least one more hour. May God bless you all in your attempts to go out and preach Jesus!

I LIKE YOUR STYLE...HOWEVER... (WRITTEN 8/21/2004)

Let's pretend you're a high school guidance counselor. Your job is to guide the young people in your school as they chart a path into adulthood. One day you're sitting in your office and Brittany, one of the school's most promising young students, knocks on your door and asks for a few minutes of your time. "Why sure," you say. "Come on in!" This particular young lady, by the way, is the head cheerleader, president of the student class, captain of the all-state girl's field hockey team, leads an after-school Bible study in her home, and has a 4.0 GPA. Who wouldn't want a whole school full of Brittany's?

She comes into your office, sits down and drills you with the most determined look you've ever seen. She then says, "I had a moment of clarity during our field hockey tournament last night. I know what I want to be when I grow up and I want you to help me plot the course that will take me there!"

You say to yourself... "Man-oh-man, I know why I became a guidance counselor...I *love* this job!"

Brittany then builds the anticipation by holding your gaze one additional second for dramatic effect and boldly announces, "I wish to be the Pope!" As cold water begins to rain down on your face and the obnoxious smell of ammonia permeates your nasal cavity, you realize that the people standing over you are attempting to bring you back into normal sinus rhythm. I'm not actually sure that's what has to happen when someone passes out but I heard it on a TV show once and thought it sounded pretty cool.

Be that as it may, this tongue-in-cheek vacation I just took from reality actually hits just a little closer to home than I'd like to admit because, in a very real sense, I find myself repeatedly trying to follow Brittany's noble, albeit misguided, path. Frankly, I would gladly trade in my airline job for one that would allow me to confidently provide for my family. Period. End of conversation. But does that career exist?

As my particular airline (UAL) has gone through the pain in recent years, I (like many of my colleagues) have been examining my options. Actually, I am truly blessed to have a lifeboat to float around in called the Air Force Reserve. Having said that, though, it really is only that—a lifeboat. I'm either going to have to climb back onto the mother ship once it's repaired, or wait for a new vessel to cruise up along side and throw down its ladder.

Frankly, I'm not too terribly worried, because I know that ultimately my future is in the infallible hands of my Heavenly Father. I do have to confront the reality, though, that He gave me a brain and expects me to use it. That opens up the possibility that, if more than one job option presents itself, I'll have to pick one. And that means I could pick one that ultimately puts me through this professional upheaval all over again someday. By the way, if you couldn't tell by now, more often than not, I'm one of those "do as I say and not as I do" Christians.

I can feel God's presence and indescribable peace one second and then, as soon as the feeling wears off, return to my previous state as a quivering ball of insecure jelly wondering if everything is going to turn out OK. I'm not terribly proud of that fact but it is, nonetheless, a fact.

Now, what have I learned about myself as I've considered my next professional step? What I've learned is that I often catch myself striving to reach the wrong goal (and perhaps you are too). I've been considering all of my options and trying to zero in on the one that will give me what UAL has not...security for my family. I keep coming full circle, though, to the glaring reality that my life on earth is a temporary gig and will *never* be secure! On more than one occasion, I've heard God say, "Hel-looooo...why are you looking to anyone or anything other than Me for security? I've already told you that you won't find it anywhere else. I'll get you the job I want you to have, and it'll allow you to buy the things your family needs. Brittany can't be the Pope, and you can't have perfect security until you join Me in Heaven, *so quit trying!*"

I don't honestly know what I'll be doing for a living one year from now, but if I've left UAL's ranks, I know that the job I go to will come with its own list of problems and shortcomings. That's just the way this program works. I don't apologize for wanting to be happy when I'm at work, and you shouldn't either. For me, there's a very good chance that that will require a job change. If you're in the same boat, try to avoid the pothole I've described as you pray, wonder and job hunt. None of us can look at job possibilities hoping that one of them will provide us with perfect security, because that doesn't exist. The only perfection this world has ever seen allowed Himself to be hung on a cross over 2000 years ago. As all of this airline turmoil has played out, I've learned to stop asking, "Why me?" Now I just want to know, "What's next?"

CHAPTER TEN

Epilogue

As we close our discussion, I would like to put one more thought on the table, so to speak. Your journey begins when you give your life to Jesus Christ. When you do that, you become a member of the body of Jesus Christ. In other words, you join a huge population of other Christians and now belong to a family. The next step is critical. I recommend you find a group of believers with whom you can fellowship and grow! Hebrews 10:24-25 says, "And let us consider how we may spur one another on toward love and good deeds. Let us not give up meeting together, as some are in the habit of doing, but let us encourage one another—and all the more as you see the Day approaching." I can't overemphasize how beneficial it will be to you when you find a good church and "plug in." Also, if you haven't already been baptized, that ought to be tops on your list!

On the subject of church attendance, there's one point I want to ask you to consider. We talked earlier about fighting against intuition and giving up overall control of our lives to the Lordship of Jesus Christ. In an almost equally intense act of deliberate, counterintuitive thinking, we can apply the same mindset to church attendance.

We normally try to join a church that somehow nourishes us with the music, clergy, and congregation that pushes all the right buttons. It's largely a "what's in it for me" thing, and we're used to attending in order to "fill the empty spiritual tank" for the coming week. As a Christian, though, your life will be in a 24/7 relationship that keeps you constantly "topped off." At least that's the way it works if you remember to keep Jesus front and center in your life. He will live in your heart, and you can't get too much more full than that! In light of that fact, church attendance can then be seen in a different light. It can become, at least in part, as much "give" as it is "get."

An example might help paint the picture. If you find out that a relative whom you haven't seen in quite some time is organizing a massive family reunion, your gut reaction would probably be excitement at the thought of "getting something" out of the experience. You're going to get to see loved ones you haven't seen in a long, long time. But what impact would your *absence* have on relatives who were so looking forward to seeing you? If you couldn't attend, they'd probably be *very* disappointed. I try to see church attendance in the same light. I do attend church in order to be nourished, encouraged, etc., but (at the risk of sounding conceited) I know my presence *can* be a blessing to others as well. That's the mindset I would like to ask you to consider.

When running into someone overly impressed with himself, I've been known to think, "Who does he think he is, God's gift to the universe?" Well, in reality, every one of us actually *is*. We're all unique and irreplaceable. Being in a congregation with other believers who are mentally, emotionally and spiritually equipped to recognize that fact is what it's all about. After all, they too are there (at least in part) to be nourished and encouraged. If you don't do that for them, who will? I truly do think that being in church in order to *add to* the collective quality of the worship experience for *everyone* is something that actually *will* put a smile on God's face!

We are actually given some insight into this dynamic through a well-known passage from scripture. 1 Corinthians 12:14-19 says "Now the body is not made up of one part but of many. If the foot should say, 'Because I am not a hand, I do not belong to the body,' it would not for that reason cease to be part of the body. And if the ear should say, 'Because I am not an eye, I do not belong to the body,' it would not for that reason cease to be part of the body. If the whole body were an eye, where would the sense of hearing be? If the whole body were an ear, where would the sense of smell be? But in fact God has arranged the parts in the body, every one of them, just as he wanted them to be. As it is, there are many parts, but one body."

Once you've been rescued from sin, God will be able to use you according to His purposes, both in *and* out of church. You will now be in a position to do what He created you to do. You can go about the business of performing the unique function in the body (yours and Christ's) that you were created to perform! If this book has done nothing more than prompt you to think along those lines and consider putting Him on the throne of your life in order to make all of that happen, then my prayers will have been answered. May God bless you!

** PRAYER OF SALVATION **

Lord Jesus,
I want to know You personally. Thank you for dying on the cross for my sins. I open the door of my life and receive You as my Savior and Lord. Thank you for forgiving me of my sins and giving me eternal life. Take control of the throne of my life. Make me the kind of person You want me to be.
Amen!

To order additional copies of this book,
please visit www.redemption-press.com.

REDEMPTION❋PRESS

CPSIA information can be obtained
at www.ICGtesting.com
Printed in the USA
FSHW02n2051080518
47805FS